VALERIE BLACK

Transforming Your Inner World

Mastering Anger, Elevating Self-Improvement, and Unleashing Your Mind's Potential

Contents

1

Chapter 1

Self-Help For Self-Improvement

2

Don't Settle for Mediocrity

Achieving genuine success requires us to steer clear of mediocrity. To do this, we must consistently strive to reach our maximum potential and enjoy life to the fullest. We can only acknowledge our accomplishments and commend ourselves for a well-done job when we put in the effort and give our best. So let us exert ourselves and always give our very best.

Success depends on self-discipline and not giving in at the first hurdle or going into a project only half-heartedly. By pushing yourself that little bit further, you will be surprised at what you can achieve. This separates the winners from the losers or the successful from the unsuccessful. That extra push toward the finish line is detrimental to this determination and by welcoming failure onto your journey, you can push through new thresholds on the way to the top.

Many people claim that they want to achieve success in life, no matter what they do, but only a few are willing to go the extra mile to reach their goals. This is why some individuals are successful in life, while others fail. It's the ones who push themselves over the thresholds that others stop at that separates those who will succeed versus those who will give up when they fail. The degree of your success is determined by your level of desire and the significance of success to you. Are you willing to succeed a little, or are you willing to go above and beyond to achieve a higher status and be outstanding?

Initially, we all have great intentions when striving to achieve our goals. We bolt out of the starting line and dash down the straight path. We see the curve and continue our stride until ahead of us we see the mountain towering over us for us to climb. Nevertheless, specific individuals experience a loss of momentum at the initial hurdle not even making it around the first curve. They fail to put in extra effort and become exhausted when things get tough. They don't pause to catch their breath and rejuvenate their energy. Had they only paced themselves, they would have had the endurance to conquer the mountain that led them to the heights they sought after.

Consequently, they give up or barely make it to the finish line, settling for second or third place at best. They believe that winning justifies their effort and don't strive to do better. On the other hand, those on a winning streak recognize the significance of going the extra mile and taking a brief break to recharge their batteries before giving it their all to cross the finish line ahead of their competitors. Such individuals are the ones who achieve genuine success in life.

Of course, all successful people don't just rely on pushing themselves. All winners have a strategy and are willing to be flexible on their way to success because life throws many obstacles into the works. We have to adapt to these unexpected happenings and not get bogged down. We must take them in our stride, run around them, and continue in the race. Proper planning makes a big difference and the ability to take risks on your road to success takes a certain mindset to ensure you'll continue past any obstacles.

Having the right set of tools in your toolbox will enable you to deal with life's obstacles more effectively and reach your goals with greater ease. In this next section, we will discuss some simple tips that will help you focus on your projects without overwhelming yourself with information, thus avoiding burnout. The aim is to encourage you to strive for excellence in your work while maintaining a healthy balance in your life.

3

Never Settle For Anything Less Than Giving It You're All

Here are some tips to help you remember never to settle for anything but your best, no matter what the project is:

1) Always put forth your best effort, regardless of project size.

You don't need to be working on the next big app idea or innovative computer program in order to have a project worthy of putting in your all. Putting time into in project of any scope ensures you are working towards the idea that will make YOU successful. Giving a project proper planning and attention ensures you are doing everything in your power to make a project flourish. Remember, failure is part of the process so don't get discouraged when your projects don't initially work out the way you want them to.

2) If you think you have given it your best shot, pause and ask yourself, "How could I improve."

After giving your project what you believe is your best effort, sit back and give yourself an evaluation. Are there areas of your work that you could have given more attention to? Are there certain aspects that you rushed over in the name of finishing the project? These details will show you which parts may need some extra attention. Try not to be the perfectionist who never releases their work because everything must be "perfect" in your eyes but strive to make sure that no stone goes overturned with the amount of effort you are putting into the whole of your project. Being able to objectively look at what you want to accomplish and giving it room to improve could be the make or break of what you aim to succeed in.

3) Plan your project, but always be willing to make changes and work around the unexpected.

Planning is essential when we are working towards a new project. Not only does it help lay out the details of what we are working on but it also gives us the space to make changes when necessary. Things don't always go as planned and we need to be able to give ourselves the flexibility to work around all unexpected events. Letting one of these events uproot your entire work will discourage you from going forward rather than figuring out what can you do to adapt to the new course your project has taken.

4) It's okay to pause but get back into the race and continue until you finish.

We've brushed over the need to take breaks in your pursuit towards success but we will touch more on the subject later in the book. What is to be said here though is that these breaks are essential when on your race. When we allow our bodies and minds time to reboot after a long sprint, we will feel rejuvenated to continue to the finish line and cross over.

5) Give Yourself a Mood Boost

We have focused on all the things to do while in the midst of creating your project but we haven't touched much on the things to do internally while you are creating your masterpiece. Making sure to take care of your mood while in the process is a key component while you are taking a pause in your work. Adapting practices like meditation and mindfulness can greatly enhance your mood while giving you time to reflect on your life. Taking time to go on a walk or sitting and enjoying a good book can all be mood boosters that can greatly help you accomplish more with your projects as well as your mental health.

4

Excellent Self-Care

While most people actively try to take care of their physical health by exercising and eating a sensible diet, most don't stop to think about the other side that completes a happy, healthy individual, their mental health.

Here are some tips for excellent self-care:

1. Treat your body – pamper it with a massage or simple stretching to ease knotted muscles after a long day.

2. Take time out – find peace and solitude by closing your eyes and practicing deep breathing, even if it's just for a few minutes.

3. Let your inner child out – engage in activities you enjoyed as a child, like rollerblading or cloud-watching.

4. Comfort yourself – indulge in activities that bring you comfort, like sitting by a fire or taking a relaxing bath surrounded by candlelight.

5. Relax in fantasy – escape into another world through books, movies, or visualization techniques.

6. Treat yourself to a mental health day – dedicate a whole day to doing activities you enjoy, without any work or guilt.

7. Rediscover nature – take a long walk through the park and appreciate the beauty of the natural world around you.

8. Do something you keep putting off – seize the day and tackle tasks you've been delaying, freeing yourself from the burden of procrastination.

These tips can help improve your mental health and contribute to a happier and healthier you. Stay mindful of your body and mind, and explore other ways to prioritize your mental well-being.

Taking Care of Yourself

Taking good care of yourself encompasses various aspects, including maintaining a healthy diet, regular exercise, and prioritizing mental well-being. When our bodies and minds are in harmony, we can experience optimal health and happiness. Here are some ways to ensure you're taking good care of yourself:

1. Express your feelings: Share your thoughts with someone you trust or jot them down in a journal to release pent-up emotions.

2. Avoid comparisons: Refrain from comparing yourself to others, as it can lead to feelings of inadequacy or envy.

3. Allocate time for yourself: Dedicate at least half an hour each day to activities you enjoy, reaffirming your self-worth.

4. Maintain a positive outlook: Find humor in challenging situations and strive to approach life with optimism.

5. Utilize relaxation techniques: Explore various methods such as reading, meditation, or exercise to alleviate stress and promote relaxation.

6. Avoid pedestals: Resist the urge to place others on pedestals, as it can lead to feelings of failure when expectations aren't met.

7. Assess work satisfaction: Reflect on your effort at work and acknowledge both the positives and negatives, striving for a balanced perspective.

8. Take breaks: Incorporate short breaks throughout the day to stretch and rejuvenate, particularly in a work setting.

9. Foster a positive attitude: Cultivate optimism by focusing on solutions rather than dwelling on problems.

10. Prioritize exercise: Incorporate physical activity into your daily routine to boost mood, enhance overall health, and alleviate stress.

11. Maintain a balanced diet: Consume a variety of nutritious

foods, emphasizing fruits and vegetables while minimizing fatty, salty, and starchy foods.

12. Journaling: Keep a journal to document your thoughts and feelings, facilitating self-reflection and personal growth.

13. Set goals: Establish achievable goals to work toward, empowering yourself to create the life you desire.

By implementing these practices into your daily life, you can enhance your overall well-being and lead a healthier, happier lifestyle. Remember, self-care is a journey, so be patient and kind to yourself along the way.

5

Tips for Getting Out of a Rut

Are you currently experiencing a feeling of being stuck in your life? Has the world suddenly seemed to have closed in around you? In addition, do you feel like you are doing the same thing day in and day out? If you feel like you're stuck in a seemingly endless cycle with no way out, chances are you're in a rut. Feeling stagnant and unmotivated can lead to depression and boredom. You gradually develop this state without being aware until you start questioning how it occurred and when it began.

For many of us, our daily life is governed by some form of routine that we cannot avoid, such as going to work 8 hours a day and taking the kids to school each morning. This is our daily life and a routine that cannot be changed for the most part. Another reason behind routine is the safety barrier; we get comfortable and feel secure in our lives, so why change? However, sometimes routine can start to get us down, leave us feeling dissociation and start causing problems in relationships, work, and daily life in general. We gradually become unhappy.

This is when a change is needed; this is the time to dig yourself out of the hole you have put yourself in and start enjoying life again.

Here are a list of tips to help you get out of a rut:

1. Do at least one daily thing different from your routine. This could be as simple as taking a short break and walking, sitting down to read a chapter of a book, or revisiting a pastime you once enjoyed.
2. Take up a new hobby and give yourself some time throughout the day to enjoy something you like doing.
3. Shake up meal times by having something different. You can try a different recipe, order different takeouts, or try foods from different cultures.
4. Get out and meet new people. You can achieve this in many ways: join a gym or club, or attend a self-improvement or hobby class.
5. Drive a different way to work or, if possible, walk or start bicycling. This will break the rut you are in and make you explore.
6. Take up a new sport; there are many types of sports, from light to more moderate forms of exercise.
7. Do something each day that is totally out of character for you. Start off with minor changes and work your way up to bigger ones.
8. If you are stuck at home with children, change your daily routine. Don't always do the same chore at the same time. Shake up the way you do your housework.
9. Make small changes around the home or work area.
10. De-clutter your home or work area; it is surprising how

being surrounded by clutter can get you down.

6

Chapter 2

Coping With Life's Challenges

7

Taking Life With a Grain of Salt

Not letting things get to you and taking life with a grain of salt is the answer to living a happy, stress-free life. When we don't realize how much stress is building up because of holding things back, worrying about things, and harboring grudges, many problems occur in life. When things are allowed to build up, we get overwhelmed, but there are many techniques that we can use to slow down, relax, and take life a little bit easier when our feelings threaten to overwhelm us.

If we don't learn to take things with a grain of salt and not worry about every little thing, and stress becomes habitual, it can severely affect our health. "Burnout" is the term commonly used, and you can burn out through problems caused by work, your lifestyle, or your personality characteristics. The symptoms of burnout can be varied, but all harm health and happiness over the long term if you don't change the situation that causes it.

8

Burn Out Symptoms

A Loss of Physical Energy

If you are continually faced with stress, then it can have a draining effect on your body and mind. This will make you feel you have less energy and can make you sluggish. You may no longer have the interests you once had or the social life you once had. Even getting out of bed may seem like too much trouble.

Frustration

Stress can result in frustration as it may cause feelings of sadness without an apparent reason, impatience, and unstable moods. These emotions can lead to losing control over one's life or feeling incapable of managing it.

Problems in Relationships

You may find that you are letting relationships slide. This could be because you lose patience with people around you, have less interest in things you used to do with others, or feel you can't mix with people you used to like being with.

A Pessimistic Outlook

When you feel burnout, it gets increasingly harder to become excited about life and what you used to do and enjoy. Your thoughts increasingly become damaging rather than positive, making it harder to look on the bright side in any situation. It becomes almost impossible to take life with a grain of salt and let even the most minor things roll off your back, and you gradually get deeper into a rut.

Tips to Avoid Burning Out

+Learn a relaxation technique such as meditation.

+Get plenty of exercise every week.

+Make sure you eat a sensible and healthy diet.

+Take time out for yourself every day.

+Learn to shrug your shoulders and cast aside anything you cannot change.

+Do something that you enjoy doing every day.

+ In a particularly stressful time, relax as best as possible, take slow deep breaths, and count to 10.

9

Dealing With Problem-Solving

All of us encounter challenges that impact our lives and require us to address them. However, how we deal with them can make all the difference. Problems can occur in life through mistakes that we make ourselves or through unforeseen circumstances beyond our control. Whichever way they cross our path, we should deal with them in the same levelheaded way.

Stay in control

There are basic ways to help ourselves overcome problems when life throws them our way, but the most important is to remain in control of our thoughts and feelings. Remember that worrying and getting upset about any situation won't change the case in any way; it won't make it go away by magic. Instead of thinking of problems as obstacles, consider these challenges by assessing how you handle and conquer them.

It is all about how we handle problems emotionally that matters. If we allow it, our emotional state can take us through our trials. If you are prone to worrying when issues arise and allow depression to set in, you still have to get through the tough times, but they will be much more complicated. First, you must understand that you don't have to understand the cause of the problem to solve it and get past it.

"If only I knew why?" This is the first question that many of us ask when faced with difficulty, but knowing why doesn't change anything. The solution to the problem lies ahead, not behind, and this is where you should be looking. Don't waste energy figuring out why; focus on finding the solution.

Allocate no more than 20% of your time dwelling on the issue and contemplating the cause; instead, dedicate 80% of your time to devising a solution for the problem. The only question you need to ask yourself is, " What will I do about it?"

When Problems Get You Down

If difficulties are getting you down, remember that every day is a new day. While life seems to be throwing many problems your way, it doesn't mean it will do so tomorrow. Leave the past where it belongs and only concentrate on the future, as it gets brighter daily.

To lift yourself up out of the blues, ask yourself, "What is happening in my life right now that I must be grateful for?" If you sit down and think deeply about this, no matter how many problems you seem to have right now, there is always something that you should be grateful for.

So dealing with solving problems is all about how you look at them and face them head-on rather than shrink from them in despair. Focus on obtaining a solution for solving the problem and then go for it full steam ahead until you have dealt with it and got through it.

10

How to Beat the Bad Day Blues

Whenever you have a bad day for whatever reason, what you need to do is think. Think hard, but not about the misery or the misfortune that has hit you. It's natural to assume that unfavorable events or experiences of the day will linger, causing emotional distress and mental anguish, depleting your emotional vitality, diminishing your zest for life, and ruining everything you cherish. In short, your negative thoughts may make your bad day seem worse than it is. Undoubtedly, that will be the case if you surrender yourself to the consequences, not otherwise.

You can devise ways to beat the bad day blues if you take control. Since negative thoughts and emotions tend to overwhelm you on a bad day, you must think of strategies to thwart them. Turn to vigorous physical workout. Or, take a long walk or go swimming. Or, just get out into the open and sit somewhere and observe the plants, trees, flowers, or the sunset, if it is sunset time. Read a delightful book, watch a funny movie, or do something that distances you from the lousy day situation, preferably both physically and, more importantly, mentally.

The Good Times

Remember the good ol' days that enriched your life in the past, all the happy experiences that elevated your spirits, and all those special friends and relatives who brought cheer and laughter into your life. Think of the good things in your life and be grateful for your blessings. Put against the bright light of your appreciation of all those better days. This single bad day or a small bunch of bad days will pale into insignificance.

Do not wallow in your bad moods and emotions because that is a way to plunge deeper into sorrow. A bad day will not become a good day by stewing over it. Remember that a bad day is just one passing day. It might have left a few scars on your mind and body, but it is essential to remember that the pain is temporary. Time is a great healer. Today, just ignore the negative aspects of the day. Instead, look at the positive side of the harmful event or happening that spoiled your day.

Are there any lessons in it for your future? How can you avoid getting into the same or similar situation? This does not mean you start thinking about your purpose in life, personal relationships, career graph, or future on a bad day. The day is unsuitable for making significant decisions about your future because such decisions cannot be sound, given the dark background. So put off making important decisions till a better day when you regain your mental poise and composure.

A straightforward formula that will help you on your bad day lies in the fact that your sorrows get divided, and your pleasures get multiplied when you share them with your close friends or confidantes. You may overcome your lousy day by discussing your problems with your close friends. Any or all of these easy-to-adopt measures will help relieve you on a bad day.

11

10 Ways To Deal With Disappointment

Dealing with disappointment is an inevitable part of life's journey, yet how we respond to it can shape our overall well-being. Here are some key strategies to help navigate and overcome disappointment when it arises:

1. **Acknowledge and Acceptance**:
   - Recognize that experiencing disappointment is a natural aspect of the human experience. Accepting this reality can alleviate some of the negative emotions associated with it.

2. **Perspective Shift**:
   - Reframe disappointment as an opportunity for growth and resilience. View it as a challenge to overcome rather than a setback.

3. **Learn and Let Go**:
   - Take time to analyze the situation and extract valuable lessons from the experience. Once learned, release any lingering negativity and focus on moving forward.

4. **Persistence and Adaptability**:
   - Maintain perseverance in pursuing your goals, even in the face of setbacks. Be willing to adjust your approach and explore alternative paths towards success.

5. **Manage Expectations**:
   - Set realistic expectations for yourself and others, recognizing that perfection is unattainable. Avoid placing undue pressure on outcomes to mitigate potential disappointment.

6. **Open Communication**:
   - Seek support from loved ones or trusted individuals by openly discussing your feelings of disappointment. Sharing your experiences can provide solace and perspective.

7. **Practice Patience**:
   - Cultivate patience as you navigate through feelings of disappointment. Allow yourself the time and space to process emotions before taking proactive steps forward.

8. **Flexibility and Adaptability**:
   - Remain adaptable in your approach to challenges, willing to explore alternative solutions and pathways towards your desired outcomes.

9. **Self-Compassion**:
   - Be kind and compassionate towards yourself during moments of disappointment. Treat yourself with the same empathy and understanding you would offer to a friend in a similar situation.

10. **Focus on the Journey**:
  - Embrace the journey of personal growth and development, recognizing that setbacks and disappointments are integral parts of the process. Stay committed to your path, knowing that each obstacle overcome brings you closer to your goals.

By integrating these strategies into your mindset and daily practices, you can develop resilience and strength in the face of disappointment, ultimately leading to greater personal fulfillment and growth.

12

8 Ways To Deal With Jealousy

Dealing with jealousy can be challenging, but it's essential to address this emotion to maintain healthy relationships. Here are some strategies to help manage jealousy effectively:

1. **Cultivate Independence**:
   - Focus on developing self-reliance and independence, rather than depending solely on others for validation or fulfillment. Invest in your personal growth and interests to build a strong sense of self-worth.

2. **Boost Confidence**:
   - Take proactive steps to boost your confidence and self-esteem. Treat yourself to activities or experiences that make you feel good about yourself, whether it's a new haircut, a spa day, or pursuing a hobby.

3. **Identify Triggers**:
   - Reflect on the specific situations or behaviors that trigger feelings of jealousy. Write them down and examine them

objectively to gain insight into your insecurities and concerns.

4. **Open Communication**:
   - Have an honest conversation with the person causing your jealousy. Express your feelings calmly and openly, focusing on finding solutions together rather than placing blame.

5. **Self-Reflection**:
   - Take time for self-reflection and introspection. Be honest with yourself about any underlying issues contributing to your feelings of jealousy, such as low self-esteem or past experiences.

6. **Rational Evaluation**:
   - Evaluate your perceptions of the person you're jealous of in a rational and balanced manner. Consider whether your feelings are based on realistic concerns or unfounded assumptions.

7. **Avoid Amplifying Emotions**:
   - Refrain from magnifying your feelings of jealousy, especially if they are fleeting or based on minor incidents. Practice self-control and mindfulness to prevent escalating emotions.

8. **Explore Self-Help Techniques**:
   - Consider exploring self-help methods such as hypnotherapy, relaxation techniques, or engaging in activities that promote calmness and emotional well-being. Experiment with different approaches to find what works best for you.

By implementing these strategies and addressing jealousy constructively, you can foster healthier relationships and cultivate a greater sense of emotional stability and security. Remember that managing jealousy is a process that requires patience, self-awareness, and ongoing effort.

13

Surviving The Winter Blues

Here are some tips for surviving the winter blues, also known as Seasonal Affective Disorder (SAD):

1. **Recognize Symptoms**:
   - Be aware of common symptoms such as sleep disturbances, overeating (especially craving carbohydrates), depression, feelings of despair, social withdrawal, lethargy, increased susceptibility to illness, and behavioral changes.

2. **Understand the Cause**:
   - Understand that SAD is believed to be linked to reduced exposure to bright light during the winter months, which affects brain chemistry. Symptoms typically start in September and peak during the darkest, coldest months.

3. **Seek Bright Light**:
   - Spend time in bright light to counteract the effects of reduced sunlight. Consider using light therapy with a light box that emits at least 2500 lux of brightness. This can help

regulate your body's internal clock and improve mood.

4. **Consider Vacationing in Brighter Climates**:
   - If possible, plan vacations to sunnier destinations during the winter months to increase exposure to natural sunlight. Even short getaways to brighter climates can have a positive impact on mood.

5. **Maintain a Healthy Lifestyle**:
   - Focus on maintaining a healthy lifestyle by eating a balanced diet, exercising regularly, and getting enough sleep. Avoid excessive consumption of comfort foods high in carbohydrates, which can contribute to weight gain and exacerbate symptoms.

6. **Practice Self-Care**:
   - Practice self-care activities that promote relaxation and well-being, such as meditation, yoga, spending time outdoors during daylight hours, and engaging in hobbies or activities you enjoy.

7. **Stay Connected**:
   - Combat social withdrawal by staying connected with friends and loved ones. Make an effort to maintain social interactions and participate in activities that bring you joy and fulfillment.

8. **Consult a Professional**:
   - If symptoms of SAD are severe or significantly impact your daily life, consider seeking professional help from a healthcare provider or mental health professional. They can offer guidance and support, as well as recommend appropriate treatment

options.

Remember that you're not alone in experiencing the winter blues, and there are resources and strategies available to help you cope and thrive during the colder months. Taking proactive steps to address symptoms and prioritize self-care can make a significant difference in managing SAD and improving overall well-being.

14

Am I Experiencing Stress?

Here are some signals that could indicate you are experiencing stress:

1. **Physical Symptoms**:
   - Feeling butterflies or knots in your stomach.
   - Experiencing cold sweats or feeling flushed and hot.
   - Dry mouth or sensation of cotton wool in your mouth.
   - Rapid heartbeat or palpitations.
   - Cold hands and trembling.
   - Difficulty concentrating and thinking clearly.
   - Unexplained feelings of dread or unease.
   - Tightness or pressure in your head, like a steel band.
   - Itchy skin or sensation of something crawling beneath the skin.
   - Disrupted sleeping patterns, including difficulty falling asleep or waking up feeling tired.
   - Decreased energy levels and lethargy, accompanied by loss of interest in activities.

2. **Short-Term vs. Long-Term Stress**:
   - Short-term stress occurs in response to specific events, such as interviews, exams, or dental appointments, and typically resolves once the event has passed.
   - Long-term stress persists over time and can lead to chronic anxiety and occasional panic attacks if left unaddressed.

3. **Managing Stress**:
   - Take steps to reduce stress in your life and find healthy ways to cope with tension.
   - Seek support from friends, family, or professionals if your stress levels are high or long-term, as you may need medication or therapy to address underlying issues.

Recognizing these signals is the first step in managing stress effectively and improving overall well-being. By addressing stressors and implementing coping strategies, you can minimize its impact on your physical and mental health.

15

Am I Experiencing Burnout?

Here are signs that you may be suffering from burnout:

1. **Physical Symptoms**:
   - Digestive issues such as stomach pain or discomfort.
   - Elevated blood pressure.
   - Persistent headaches.
   - Teeth grinding.
   - Chronic fatigue and exhaustion.
   - Increased risk of heart problems, including heart attacks and strokes.

2. **Emotional and Mental Symptoms**:
   - Feelings of hopelessness and powerlessness.
   - Emotional detachment or dissociation.
   - Decreased satisfaction with work and life in general.
   - Building resentment towards work or life circumstances.
   - Sense of being trapped in a rut with no way out.
   - Withdrawal from social interactions and isolation.
   - Feelings of incompetence and failure.

3. **Preventive Measures**:
   - Prioritize your physical health by undergoing regular check-ups and maintaining a balanced diet.
   - Incorporate regular exercise into your routine to manage stress and improve overall well-being.
   - Ensure you get an adequate amount of sleep each night to support your body's recovery and resilience.
   - Learn and practice relaxation techniques, such as deep breathing or meditation, to cope with stress effectively.

Recognizing these signs early and taking proactive steps to manage stress can help prevent burnout and promote better overall health and well-being. It's essential to prioritize self-care and seek support from healthcare professionals if needed to address burnout symptoms effectively.

16

Should I Leave My Relationship?

Here are the top 10 signs that it may be time to leave a relationship:

1. Increased arguing: If disagreements and arguments become more frequent, especially over minor issues, it could indicate underlying problems in the relationship.

2. Decreased passion: A noticeable decline in intimacy and sexual activity without a clear reason might signal a loss of connection between partners.

3. Avoidance: If you and your partner start avoiding spending time together or engaging in meaningful interactions, it could signify growing distance and disinterest.

4. Jealousy: Deliberate attempts by your partner to make you jealous or seeking attention from others may indicate feelings of insecurity or a lack of commitment.

5. Interference from family: Involving family members in conflicts or using them against each other can escalate tensions and strain the relationship.

6. Growing dependency: A sudden increase in your partner's reliance on you may indicate underlying issues or a fear of losing the relationship.

7. Anxiety or depression: Significant changes in your partner's mood or mental health, especially without an apparent cause, could be a sign of relationship distress.

8. Expecting change: Unrealistic expectations for you to change or dissatisfaction with who you are may signal deeper dissatisfaction within the relationship.

9. Increased time away: Spending more time apart, whether at work or with friends, may suggest a desire for space or avoidance of relationship issues.

10. Secrecy: If your partner becomes secretive or starts hiding things from you, such as communication devices or online activities, it may indicate a breach of trust or emotional detachment.

Recognizing these signs and addressing underlying issues is crucial for determining the future of the relationship and prioritizing your well-being and happiness. If these signs persist and efforts to resolve them prove futile, it may be time to consider ending the relationship for your own emotional health and fulfillment.

Please note that the information provided is intended to encourage readers to explore their understanding of relationship dynamics and personal triggers. It is meant to assist individuals in fostering healthier relationships with themselves and others by gaining insight into potential signs of relationship challenges. The material presented is for informational purposes only and should not replace professional advice or therapy. It is advisable to seek guidance from qualified professionals for personalized support and guidance in addressing specific relationship concerns or emotional issues.

Chapter 3

Anger And Happiness

18

Trigger Trips And Aids

When you're calm, make a list of things, people, places, events, etc., that tend to trip your trigger:

+Calling businesses and getting automated menus to choose from that run you in circles, accomplishing nothing productive.
   +Handling angry customer service calls.
   +Going to visit your in-laws.
   +Heavy traffic during rush hour.
   +Losing my Mutual Funds account in the stock market.
   +Ect.

Anger Aids

+List ways to deal with anger when you have a positive frame of mind and are in an excellent mood to spark better creativity:
   +Cool off with ice cream – As simplistic as this sounds, something calm and soothing can often help take the heat off the moment and begin cooling the entire body down.
   +Take a hike or walk – Taking a step back, away from it all,

can give you a better worldview of the situation. Being at the center of issues can make them seem more significant than they are, making the proverbial mountains out of molehills.

+Dance – Let it all out via your expression. Dance to the beat of the music of your choice.

+Write it out - Journal and create a column for 'lemons' and another for solutions or 'lemonade.'

+Avoid/alter the path of destruction in advance – Take a different route during rush hour or alter your schedule.

+By planning, you can prepare yourself in advance. Plan and conquer, and keep at the process regularly.

19

The Top 10 Ways of Controlling Anger

1. **Recognize the Negative Impact of Anger**: Everyone experiences anger at some point, but it's crucial to understand that it leads to negative emotions like sadness, guilt, and frustration, hindering happiness and prosperity.

2. **Identify the Source of Anger**: Determine whether you're upset about someone's actions or your reaction to them. Understanding what triggers your anger is essential for finding a resolution.

3. **Practice Anger Management**: The more you practice controlling your anger, the easier it becomes to let go and move on, empowering you to take control of your life and happiness.

4. **Relaxation Techniques**: When anger builds up, consciously relax your body and breathe deeply from the diaphragm to calm both body and mind, facilitating the release of anger before it escalates.

5. **Assess the Situation's Impact**: Evaluate whether getting angry and agitated will make any difference in the situation. Consider whether the stress is worth it and whether reacting angrily will change anything.

6. **Visualize a Peaceful Place**: Create a mental oasis where you feel relaxed and calm, enabling you to retreat to this stress-free zone when anger begins to build up.

7. **Empathy and Perspective-Taking**: Put yourself in the other person's shoes and consider how you would react if you were in their position. This can provide insight into the situation and alleviate anger.

8. **Take Responsibility**: Acknowledge that you alone allow anger to affect you. While someone else may trigger it, you have the power to let it go and not let it control you.

9. **Counting and Distraction**: Counting to ten can help diffuse anger by diverting your focus from the triggering event and consciously releasing the anger.

10. **Affirmations and Mantras**: Repeat positive affirmations or mantras to yourself when anger starts to build, such as "I feel calm and relaxed" or "anger isn't going to get me anywhere." This can help shift your mindset and promote a more positive and calming perspective.

20

Turning Hate Into Good

How often have we said to ourselves, "I hate this or that," or even " I hate him/her," but where does hate get us? Does it make us feel any better to declare we hate something or somebody? Hate is a negative feeling and negative emotions only bring about bad. When we think of the word hate, we start thinking of coldness towards others or something.

We automatically isolate ourselves from that person or situation; nothing good can come from such feelings. There are many types of hate, such as racial, sexual, ethnicity, or just plain disliking a situation or disliking a position due to a phobia. Here are some ways to think about turning the hatred into a more positive and reasonable approach.

Racial Hate

People are people. We are all flesh and blood. Whatever the color of our skin or our background in life. We all have the same shade of blood flowing through our veins; we have the same shape, hearts, and brains. We all have fingers, toes, and the ability to communicate. Why do so many people profess to hate someone else just because they have a different skin color or come from a foreign country?

It is worth remembering that underneath, we are all the same and want the same out of life for ourselves and our families. There are good and bad people of all colors and nationalities in life. So instead of hating someone because they look different from you, look deeper inside than the skin color and see the true person.

Sexual Hate

What difference does a person's sexual preference make to the person that they are? Many people hate others solely based on their sexual preference, but why? For example, you could meet someone by chance and enjoy their company, laughing, talking, and having a good time until you discover they are gay.

Suddenly, your feelings alter towards this person, yet nothing has changed substantially from a few minutes ago. The person hasn't changed; they are still the same person you were having fun with and liked being with, yet this simple point changes everything. Maybe it is just a matter of ethics, how you were brought up, and what you were brought up to believe in, but why can't you change your thoughts and feelings? Why can't you allow yourself to continue having fun and enjoying being with that person? If they were a good person before the admittance of their sexual preference, then they still are now.

Hate Due to a Phobia

People can hate certain situations or objects in life due to an extreme phobia; this could be a hate of heights, spiders, snakes, the dentist, or being enclosed in elevators. This type of hate is brought about by fear, a deep fear of something or a situation over which those affected have hardly or no control. However, since fear is all about feelings and thoughts, fear and hate of this type can be controlled by the mind with some help and know-how. An analyst can help to turn this type of hate and fear into a more positive outlook and help the person overcome the phobia and turn a fearful situation into a good one.

21

About Anger

Nearly anyone and everyone – people of all ages worldwide – is prone to displays of anger. The degree of frequency and intensity of the emotion vary most and most often results in how well a person handles the anger and whether there are positive or negative results. A key to those who successfully manage anger is gaining control. To gain control over the emotion, it helps first to look at anger itself, what it is, and how to deal with it effectively.

Anger is an emotion. It can be triggered by various things, issues, people, places, etc. Some of the top triggers are jealousy, confrontations, failure, greed, fear, low self-esteem, assertiveness, feeling threatened, and pain. When a person gets angry, the negative emotion can harm the person's physical and emotional well-being. The heart rate increases, stress levels rise, and often a fight or flight reaction is the immediate response, neither one always presenting a healthy alternative.

What works best for managing anger is to be prepared in

advance to learn primary triggers, how to tell when they are about to happen, and how to avoid them when possible, as well as a variety of coping skills to deal with what is necessary. Keep a private journal to note any anger triggers, ways to avoid confrontations, and possible coping techniques. You can use the following triggers, coping techniques, and helpful tips as a starting point.

22

What Does Happiness Mean?

Do you feel something is missing from your life? Do you think the world is against you or that other people seem to smile, laugh, and be much happier and contented than you are? Have you ever stopped to wonder why this might be?

Moreover, what can you do about it? Have you ever considered what happiness is? Happiness and contentment in life differ for all of us. What makes one person happy doesn't necessarily bring contentment to another. We are often satisfied in life but don't realize it. Very often, the hustle and bustle of life can completely overtake all else, leaving us little time to enjoy the things that make us smile and enjoy life to the fullest.

If you stop and sit down and think about what makes you happy and feel contented, you might discover you already have those things around you, but you just didn't realize it. However, sometimes we can get into a slump and haven't yet come across the conditions that we regard as bringing happiness and contentment. If this is the case, you have to figure out what changes you need to make to bring happiness.

In most cases, minor things bring happiness, and you have the power to gain them by working toward them. Your happiness and contentment depend entirely on you; no one else can give them to you. It is something inside you that you have to find and work towards. You can either stop in the rut or take positive action and make changes to your life or yourself to accomplish contentment.

To understand what happiness means to you, the first step you should take is to look at your emotions and ask yourself questions such as "If I could be enjoying something in my life, what would it be?" and "What makes me feel contented in my life right now?" Once you understand your vision of happiness and contentment, you can build on what you have now or focus on changing your life to what you would like it to be.

The critical thing to remember is to examine your feelings through the answers you give to your questions, examine them honestly, and concentrate on the good or bad feelings you get from your questions and answers.

No magic spell or potion can bring you contentment and happiness. It is already right there inside of you. All you have to do is recognize, develop, and bring it out to start enjoying life. Happiness can be found in family life, work, relationships, nature, or a pet, to name just a few. It can be found in anything and any situation if you just know where to look and look in the right direction, the inner you.

Developing Relationships for Happiness

Learning to develop your relationship skills can significantly affect your life and your happiness. We all have relationships, whether marriage, living together, sons, daughters, friends, or family. Having a good relationship with them makes a big difference.

The biggest downfall in relationships is poor communication. Communicating poorly in a relationship leads to misunderstandings, disagreements, and anger and eventually disturbs your relationship. Improving your communication in relationships can help you develop a more profound, lasting, meaningful relationship and much happier life.

There are many tips and techniques which are quick and easy to learn to get more out of your relationships and develop them into more meaningful ones. Here are just a few.

1. **Avoid Bringing Up Past Issues**: When dealing with conflicts, focus on the present issue rather than dredging up past grievances. This approach leads to greater clarity and increases the chances of finding a resolution.

2. **Practice Empathy**: Try to understand the other person's perspective during conflicts. Mutual understanding fosters compromise and facilitates problem-solving, whereas a one-sided focus on personal views hinders progress.

3. **Active Listening**: Truly listen to what the other person is saying without drifting off or formulating your response

prematurely. Genuine listening promotes understanding and strengthens communication.

4. **Resist Defensiveness**: When criticized, refrain from becoming defensive. Instead, strive to comprehend the other person's viewpoint, even if it's difficult to hear.

5. **Seek Compromise**: Rather than stubbornly pursuing victory in arguments, explore opportunities for compromise. Collaborative problem-solving yields better outcomes than adversarial approaches.

6. **Take Breaks When Necessary**: If discussions become heated, take a break to cool off. Continuing while emotions are high risks saying hurtful things that may be regretted later.

7. **Accept Imperfection**: Acknowledge that nobody is perfect and refrain from placing blame solely on the other person. Recognizing one's own fallibility promotes humility and understanding.

8. **Seek Counseling if Needed**: If relationship issues persist, don't hesitate to seek professional counseling. Seeking help demonstrates commitment to resolving problems and improving the relationship.

9. **Prioritize Quality Time**: Dedicate time to nurture relationships, such as taking walks together to facilitate meaningful conversations rather than passive activities like watching TV.

10. **Express Thoughtfulness**: Make unexpected gestures to

show you care, such as surprising loved ones with a phone call simply to say hello.

11. **Show Appreciation**: Occasionally, express appreciation for your loved ones with tokens of gratitude or gestures to make them feel special.

12. **Express Affection**: In loving relationships, openly communicate your feelings and demonstrate affection through physical gestures like holding hands during conversations.

23

How to Make Every Day a Great One

The key to enjoying life and making the most of every day is to notice the little things in life that happen all around us, take a moment and slow down, relax, and enjoy every precious minute throughout the day. Today's world is filled with hustle and bustle. People are rushing here, there, and everywhere without a minute to spare. We have more technological advancements to help in our lives, yet we still don't seem to have a minute to spare for ourselves.

It's possible that modern technological advancements, such as computers, video games, and streaming TV, have caused us to overlook the value of simple pleasures like having meaningful conversations, sharing meals with loved ones, and taking a leisurely stroll. To make the most out of each day and find genuine enjoyment, it's crucial to slow down, unwind, and focus on our own needs and desires, including what brings us happiness and contentment.

In order to get the most out of every day, you have to start with yourself. You must look after yourself, eat a healthy diet, exercise, get enough sleep, and take care of yourself in general. Having a daily schedule is also a necessity. By planning a daily schedule, you are to give yourself some "me" time. We all need time to enjoy doing what we like, be it listening to music, taking a walk, a long hot soak in the tub, or a hobby.

So what can we do to ensure we get the most out of every day? Here are some tips to help you.

Forgive Yourself

If, at the end of your day, you didn't accomplish all that you set out to do, then forgive yourself and say to yourself, "I did the best I possibly could and made the most of today. Tomorrow is a brand new day."

Don't beat yourself up about minor things you didn't accomplish, and worry about it. There's always tomorrow; as long as you make the most of today, that's all that matters.

Your Daily To-Do List

We all have certain chores that must be done daily. Do these chores in order of importance, and don't let them pile up. However, sing along to the radio while you do the dishes and dance with the vacuum as you push it around the house. Take pleasure in doing mundane chores and turn them into an enjoyable experience instead of moaning and grumbling about having to do them.

Take Regular Breaks

Whether at home or work, give yourself a break now and again, even if it is only for 5 minutes. Learn a quick relaxation technique and unwind if you feel tense. If at work, then get up and stretch your legs or grab a cup of coffee and say hello with a smile to everyone you pass on your way to the coffee machine.

Do Something You Enjoy Doing.

Make it a point to set aside time just for you to do what you want. This could be reading, taking a bubble bath, meditating, going to the gym, or anything you enjoy doing that makes you feel good and puts a smile on your face.

Positive Thinking:

Try to have a positive attitude towards life even when things aren't going how you want them to. Look for the good in the situation and what you can learn from it rather than looking at it negatively.

24

Stay Happy: Don't Hold Onto Grudges

By keeping grudges, we are holding onto the past, which holds us back and stops us from growing and going onward with our lives. Grudges and refusing to let go of the past are negative. Negativity holds us back, prevents us from achieving what we can, and encourages resentment, unhappiness, and fear instead of being happy and finding peace within ourselves.

Forgiveness is the key to happiness. True forgiveness is when you can release all your negative feelings towards another and let them go completely. You have to let the grudge go not only through words of acceptance but also feel it in your heart and soul.

Why Is Forgiving So Difficult to Do?

Our negative ego causes us to hold a grudge and tells us not to let it go. Like everything that blocks success and happiness, negativity again plays a huge part, but this time, it affects our ego. By letting negativity affect our lives this way, we open the door and welcome bitterness and deep resentment, manifesting deep within us and showing themselves in our health.

Holding onto a grudge causes ulcers, stress, and overall poor health, so we must learn to let go of our resentment and move on with life by letting go of our grudges. As with every other problem relating to negativity, it is all about how we think. Forgiveness is all about letting go of harmful train of thought patterns and developing new ones.

Developing the Ability to Let Go

Developing the ability to let go takes time. If you allow yourself to look at your feelings honestly and calmly, you will realize that negative feelings evaporate, and you begin to feel peace of mind by letting go of deep resentment. The key to genuinely forgiving is first being able to release the hurt and anger that person has caused you. Without letting go of these feelings, true forgiveness is next to impossible. Suppose you try to forgive without releasing the emotions. The anger you feel will only continue to build and manifest as resentment further down the road, and resentment will, without a doubt, eventually rear its ugly head.

A great way of releasing your feelings is to look directly at them and, in great detail, admit what has hurt you and why it hurt you and realize why you must let it go. Look at your feelings in a different light and gradually allow yourself to forgive and let go.

Forgiveness has to come from deep within you. There is no outside force that keeps a grudge building up. The feelings of forgiveness can only be generated from within yourself. Only you can take responsibility, forgive, let go, and move on to a more peaceful and contented life.

25

Success and Happiness Are Not Always Material

When most people think of happiness and being successful, they think of owning big houses, fast cars, expensive designer clothes, and how big a bank balance you have. However, your success and happiness do not necessarily depend on the material things you have in life. If you are happy in life with what you have, regardless of the material possessions that you own or don't own, then you are a very wealthy and successful person indeed.

It is very often the smallest things in life that are priceless but are not of any great value other than to the person who cherishes them for one reason or another. These can be photographs, cards, a song, or even memories that can be precious to an individual.

In a society where we have been brought up believing material possessions are what is important, it can be hard to believe that owning material possessions isn't what makes us happy and brings success. How common it is to hear someone say, "If only I had this or that, I would be the happiest person on earth." However, when we get what it is we wish for, we are never satisfied and only begin to dream and wish we had something better. The newness of having a material possession soon wears off, and this pattern continues throughout most people's lives. This is perhaps easier to realize if you remember when you were a child. Your parents would spend hundreds of dollars on birthdays and Christmas presents because you had to have that "special" toy, but how quickly they were discarded when something new came onto the scene. The same applies to wealth. Regardless of how much money you have, do you believe you have?

Would having a bank account with thousands of dollars make such a difference in your life? Would it bring you any more happiness or success than you have now? We all want to live a comfortable life without struggling each month to pay bills. That's only natural, but apart from that, money doesn't bring true happiness and success. You can have thousands in the bank, but if you're alone in life, without real friends and family, without love, then you can never find true happiness and success.

What Are Success and Happiness?

To determine actually what success and happiness mean, you should first ask yourself this.

1. What is the meaning of success and happiness?
2. What does it mean to be truly successful and happy?
3. What do I want out of life?

These are the core questions behind understanding what happiness and success would mean to you as an individual, for happiness and success mean different things to each of us. You can be rich and successful in many more ways than having material possessions and money. Think about some of the things you have in your life now. Are you one of the richest and most successful people on the earth?

1. **True Friends**: Having five genuine friends who stand by you through all circumstances is invaluable wealth.

2. **Health**: Prioritizing good health through proper nutrition and regular exercise surpasses the importance of financial wealth.

3. **Family**: Being surrounded by a loving family ensures a fulfilling and joyous life, contributing to success and contentment.

4. **Good Character**: Possessing traits like honesty, kindness, and integrity leads to unparalleled success and fulfillment in life.

26

Chapter 4

Change For Good

27

Changing Bad Habits Into Good Ones

All of us possess habits, and among them are the negative ones. Although challenging, it is worth the effort to transform bad habits into positive ones by adopting a determined mindset. Our practices can significantly impact our lives, affecting our thoughts and emotions. Damaging habits can undermine our self-worth, leading to pessimism, while positive habits can foster a sense of achievement, accomplishment, and optimism. So, how can we effectively break and replace bad habits? Below are some valuable techniques that can assist you in turning negative patterns into positive ones.

1. **List Reasons to Stop Your Habit**:
   - Identify all the reasons why you want to quit your habit, such as financial costs, health consequences, and social impacts. Writing down these reasons provides clarity and motivation for change.

2. **Self-Analysis**:
   - Reflect on what you gain from your habit. Determine if it

aligns with your desires and if it truly brings enjoyment, or if it's merely a familiar pattern you're hesitant to break.

3. **List Positive Replacements**:
   - Consider alternative activities or habits that would be more beneficial. Examples include hobbies, exercise, reading, learning new skills, or spending quality time with loved ones. These substitutes can distract from the habit and promote positive lifestyle changes.

4. **Visualization**:
   - Envision the benefits and improvements that breaking your habit would bring. Visualize yourself experiencing better health, improved surroundings, increased productivity, and enhanced relationships as a result of healthier choices.

5. **Take One Day at a Time**:
   - Focus on tackling your habit one day at a time rather than worrying about the future. Set a quit date and commit to it, regardless of challenges that may arise. Keeping a journal can aid in processing emotions and tracking progress throughout the journey of breaking the habit.

6. **Seek Support**:
   - Reach out to friends, family, or support groups who can provide encouragement and accountability as you work to overcome your habit. Having a strong support system can make the journey easier and more successful.

7. **Identify Triggers and Coping Mechanisms**:
   - Recognize the situations, emotions, or cues that trigger your

habit, and develop healthy coping strategies to address them. This may involve practicing relaxation techniques, engaging in mindfulness activities, or seeking professional guidance.

8. **Celebrate Milestones**:
   - Acknowledge and celebrate your achievements along the way, whether it's one day, one week, or one month without engaging in the habit. Rewarding yourself for progress can reinforce positive behavior and motivate continued efforts.

9. **Stay Persistent and Patient**:
   - Breaking a habit takes time and effort, so be patient with yourself throughout the process. Stay committed to your goal, even if you experience setbacks or challenges. With persistence and determination, lasting change is achievable.

28

Turning Change Into Choice!

Change happens in our lives naturally, whether we like it or not. Day turns into night. We grow older, as do our children. We buy houses, change homes, lifestyles, jobs, and more. Some of us don't handle change as well as others. You see others happy to change careers and relationships or move to another home. You wonder why they are so happy. What is it that is so exciting about change? And why do you only fear change?

Unfortunately, fear can be a paralyzing emotion and feeling. It can make us afraid to do anything, and we stand still. The biggest fear of all humans is the fear of the unknown. When we can't predict the outcome, we usually become afraid. Most of the time, we can't predict the outcome of any change. That can be scary. However, one of the things in life that will happen is change.

How to Handle 'Change' Better

But fear not! There is a better way to handle change so that it's not so scary. The reality is that difference is not so much about handling something new and different as it is about making the new and different things a choice – owning them as your own. The best way to conquer your fear of these new things or changes is by taking control, having a positive mindset, and taking charge in a manner that says it is your choice to change. Make this a conscious decision – take ownership of the facts.

Planning for Change

Let's say you need to make a career change. Plan out everything. How many interviews will you do a day? How will you obtain those interviews? Will you be switching to a different career or staying in the same type of career? What do you want to do? Where do you see yourself in six months? Answer these questions in a notebook or journal. Then, outline what you plan on doing. Now most of the unknown is known! You have taken ownership of your change and hold the controls.

Don't stop there, not even after you make your career change. Set long-term and short-term goals for yourself. The best way to conquer a fear is to face it and do it often. If you do this regularly, you will soon wonder what made you so nervous. Make change your choice!

Additionally, get help regularly from the pros by checking out library and online books, audio recordings, videos, and other helpful information focused on motivation and inspiration to learn more about how successful people have accepted and taken charge of the changes in their lives.

29

Improving Your Emotional Well-Being

Many things in life can affect our emotional well-being, which is one of the most important aspects of being healthy. To be truly healthy, having stable and healthy emotions is essential. If your feelings are unstable, your whole body will be affected, leading to a decline in health and overall well-being. If you follow the holistic belief of health, this dictates that along with healthy eating, exercise, and dieting, we have to take care of our mental health.

We gain proper overall health only when the body and mind are fit and healthy. Emotional, physical, intellectual, and social well-being all come together. If any of these are affected, it will affect our health. Many factors can affect these, including problems in relationships, unemployment, money problems, social problems, and physical problems, to name but just a few. Improving your emotional well-being depends on altering aspects of your life that affect it.

Stress is the biggest enemy that can change our emotions and feelings, so you must remove as much stress from your daily life as possible. You should learn new techniques to banish stress quickly and effortlessly without allowing it to build up. You can choose many strategies to combat stress, from practicing yoga and meditation to simple breathing exercises and affirmations. The key is to find the method that works best for you.

Many of us develop negative thinking patterns over time, which can impact our emotional well-being. Constantly expecting the worst or criticizing ourselves can result in low self-confidence and self-esteem. One way to combat negative thoughts and emotions is through positive affirmations or self-talk. Changing our thoughts can change how we feel about ourselves and our lives, leading to a healthier outlook and overall well-being.

Situations that occur in your daily life can change your emotional well-being. While we often cannot change conditions, we can change how we deal with them and how they affect our thoughts, feelings, and emotions. Feelings of anger, sadness, and uncertainty cause problems with our emotional well-being and overall health. The trick is not to hold your feelings inside but to let them out. Harboring anger, resentment, or sadness for long periods can devastate our emotional well-being. Keeping a journal to write about your thoughts and feelings can help, as can having someone to talk to; the main point is getting your feelings out.

Key points to improving your emotional well-being:

1. **Learning to Relax and Let Go of Stress**:

- Practice relaxation techniques such as deep breathing, meditation, or mindfulness to reduce stress levels and promote emotional balance.

2. **Maintaining a Sensible Diet and Regular Exercise**:
   - Prioritize nutrition and physical activity to support overall well-being. Eating healthily and staying active can positively impact mood and mental health.

3. **Ensuring Quality Sleep Every Night**:
   - Establish a consistent sleep schedule and create a conducive sleep environment to enhance sleep quality. Sufficient rest is essential for emotional resilience and cognitive function.

4. **Addressing Problems Promptly**:
   - Confront challenges and conflicts as they arise rather than avoiding or suppressing them. Seeking solutions and support can prevent issues from escalating and negatively impacting emotional health.

5. **Being Kind to Yourself**:
   - Practice self-compassion and avoid self-criticism. Give yourself permission to make mistakes and acknowledge your worth irrespective of imperfections.

6. **Expressing Thoughts and Feelings**:
   - Share your thoughts and emotions with trusted individuals or through journaling. Processing and verbalizing feelings can alleviate emotional burdens and foster a sense of relief.

7. **Engaging in Enjoyable Activities Daily**:

- Incorporate activities that bring joy and fulfillment into your daily routine. Engaging in hobbies, spending time with loved ones, or pursuing interests can uplift mood and enhance overall well-being.

30

7 Simple Steps to Stop Procrastinating:

1. **Plan Your Daily Activities**:
   - Create a to-do list either on paper or digitally to organize your tasks for the day.

2. **Prioritize Your Tasks**:
   - Rank your activities based on importance and urgency, ensuring that critical tasks are completed first.

3. **Estimate Time Needed**:
   - Evaluate the complexity of each task and allocate realistic time frames to avoid underestimation or overestimation.

4. **Organize Your Life**:
   - Establish discipline in your daily routine to prevent wasting time and minimize distractions. Keep personal belongings in designated places to save time searching for them.

5. **Start Small**:
   - Break down daunting tasks into smaller, manageable steps to alleviate feelings of overwhelm. Begin with a small step, gradually progressing toward the larger goal.

6. **Prioritize Early in the Day**:
   - Tackle the most important tasks first thing in the morning to prevent procrastination from setting in. Avoid delaying crucial tasks, as procrastination can become a habit over time.

7. **Manage Mental Well-being**:
   - Practice self-care techniques to cope with anxiety, depression, and stress, which can contribute to procrastination. Incorporate mental relaxation methods such as meditation to maintain emotional balance and focus.

31

New Year's Resolutions You Can Keep

Do you know most people who make resolutions on the eve of a new year break them within the first three or four months? Do you know why? If you do, you won't make impractical resolutions. If you don't, you might ask what resolutions you can keep or how to make only those resolutions that will work for a long time. The answer is simple. Be realistic, not idealistic, in making your resolutions. If your goals are too high to reach, you are bound to give up your attempt halfway through rather than stick to your resolution.

Anyone can make a halfhearted resolution for the New Year. What is complex and requires commitment is to keep it. To overcome the hurdles and sustain your resolutions, you need to brainstorm. Think about all the possible restrictions that the New Year's resolutions will impose on you. Think about all the changes that you must make to have successful resolutions.

If you want to stop smoking completely, think of the steps you will take to resist the temptation when you are alone or in a company. Ask yourself whether you will enforce self-discipline to reduce the habit gradually in stages and reach the final goal set as per the time frame you chalked out for yourself. Monitor your progress periodically and devise corrective measures wherever necessary. That way, you can monitor yourself to follow your resolutions.

Get Others Involved

Another way to keep your resolutions is to tell your family and friends about them and seek their active help and support. You should never depend on your plan but seek the consent of others. You may have all the discipline and motivation in the world, but you will receive unmatched support from loved ones when trying hard to do something. This external encouragement will help support and reinforce your efforts.

Don't get disheartened if you occasionally deviate from your chosen path. Don't let any of your minor slips and setbacks fill you with guilt feeling severe enough to make you drop your resolutions. Even if that happens, start again more vigorously, this time with a better action plan and follow-up program.

Consider striving to achieve and maintain some of the following New Year's Resolutions aimed at enhancing your overall well-being:

1. **Focus on Health**:
   - Eat a substantial breakfast rich in fruits and vegetables.
   - Maintain regular meal times.
   - Stay hydrated by drinking fruit juice, milk, and plenty of

water.
   - Incorporate simple fitness activities like walking, yoga, or outdoor sports.

2. **Break Addictions**:
   - Kick habits such as tobacco, caffeine, excessive food or drink consumption, and pornography.

3. **Prioritize Family Time**:
   - Dedicate regular intervals to spend quality time with your family, whether daily or weekly.

4. **Continual Learning**:
   - Cultivate new hobbies or interests to stimulate personal growth and development.

5. **Expand Mental Horizons**:
   - Engage in activities like reading, crosswords, or Sudoku puzzles to broaden your intellectual capabilities.

These are just a few examples of popular resolutions to consider. Customize your resolution according to your preferences and needs, whether it's simple or intricate, to foster personal growth and well-being.

32

Don't Let Addictions Control Your Life

First, have you even realized you need to break free from your addictions? If not, now is the time to make a conscious decision about regaining control by trying to kick your harmful habit NOW. You can't wait for an opportune moment forever because it will never come if you don't want it.

Once you decide to quit, make your decision public. Tell your family, your friends, and everybody and anybody interested in your well-being about it. By doing so, you are making it rather difficult to back out. You may also let them know you're looking for their support for your decision. It is important to openly enlist their help and cooperation to help kick your bad habit.

Avoid getting into situations full of temptations. No matter how strong you are, the temptation will be overwhelming. When you try to give up smoking, for instance, hanging out with your chain-smoker friends will do you no good. Don't accept invitations to a party when you know you will be subjected to peer or situational pressure to take the very things you are trying never to use. If you do, you will never come out of your compulsive weakness for a drug, drink, smoke, or habit you have decided to kick.

You May Need Professional Help

If you find yourself struggling with long-term dependency on substances like alcohol, drugs, tobacco, or pornography, seeking professional assistance alongside support from loved ones may be necessary. Specialists will conduct a thorough assessment of your situation and devise a tailored program for you to adhere to under their guidance for a designated duration.

Several support groups may join in. Following the rehabilitation program is key to getting yourself back on track. Ultimately, your will is the only thing that can get rid of the addiction for good. People under some stress or tension wrongly believe they can calm themselves and feel relaxed if they use tobacco or alcohol, or drugs.

They first try to drown their sorrows in addictive substances and habits detrimental to their health but end up drenched in their addictions. If only you realized the futility of seeking relief from your grief in addictions, you would never risk damaging your health, losing your wealth, and destroying whatever happiness you have had so far. There are better ways to confront and conquer your problems than giving in to addiction.

Outlets For Addiction

Learn to relax and rebuild your physical and mental reserves by doing regular physical exercise, yoga, meditation, or taking to hobbies by exploiting your creative interests. Instead of attempting to escape from reality through the door that addictions seem to open for you, learn to adopt a positive attitude, face the inevitable, and overcome the consequences with courage.

You Are in Control

Remember, there are few quick-fix solutions to life's problems. Likewise, there are no easy ways to overcome your addictions. Only concerted efforts on your part will help you in the end. Take control by training your mind to face life's tough challenges.

33

Chapter 5

Healthy Communication

34

Developing Healthy Communication Skills

Good communication skills are essential in all walks of life and different situations. Relationships rely on good communication to survive and strengthen. How you live among your neighbors requires good communication. In your work, doing well in school or college, and dealing with difficult people are just ways excellent communication skills can help in life.

Most of us have to deal with difficult people at some stage or another, so we must know how to deal with them effectively to get the best outcome. If you face difficulties as a standard part of your daily life, it will gradually affect your life. Experiencing nervousness, anxiety, and stress can be expected when facing challenges in life. While removing the source of the problem may seem like the easiest solution, it may only sometimes be possible, especially if the issue involves a colleague or a loved one. If this is the case, you have to develop strategies to help you develop healthier communication between you and them. Here are some tips to help you:

Here are several strategies to navigate interactions with difficult individuals in your daily life:

1. **Avoid Controversial Topics**:
   - Steer clear of discussing personal matters like religion or politics to prevent potential conflicts. If you sense tension escalating, redirect the conversation or excuse yourself from the situation.

2. **Focus on Adaptation, Not Change**:
   - Attempting to change a difficult person may lead to defensiveness and further conflict. Instead, adjust your responses and perceptions, setting clear boundaries when necessary.

3. **Practice Empathy**:
   - Strive to understand the other person's perspective, acknowledging that neither party is always right. Seek to find common ground and empathize with their viewpoint.

4. **Highlight Positive Attributes**:
   - Emphasize the positive qualities of the individual, especially if they are a family member. Recognizing their strengths can foster better relationships.

5. **Acceptance**:
   - Accept the person for who they are, including both their strengths and flaws. Set realistic expectations and avoid trying to change fundamental aspects of their personality.

6. **Establish Boundaries**:
   - Recognize when it's necessary to distance yourself from the

individual and take action accordingly. Setting and enforcing boundaries is crucial for maintaining your well-being.

7. **Avoid Blame**:
   - Refrain from assigning blame during negative interactions, focusing instead on finding solutions and maintaining civility.

8. **Politeness as a Last Resort**:
   - In extreme cases, maintaining polite behavior may be the most realistic expectation. Sometimes, despite efforts, incompatible personalities may prevent deeper connections.

9. **Maintain Your Sense of Humor**:
   - Retain your sense of humor when dealing with difficult individuals, allowing you to navigate challenging situations with grace and levity.

10. **Surround Yourself with Positivity**:
   - Cultivate positive relationships to counterbalance the impact of negative interactions. Having a supportive network can provide emotional resilience.

These strategies, combined with improved communication skills and stress management techniques, can help make interactions with difficult individuals more manageable in your daily life.

35

10 Tips for Effective Communication:

1. **Practice Active Listening**:
   - Allow the speaker to finish before responding to ensure you grasp their full message. Interrupting can be perceived as disrespectful and may cause you to miss important points.

2. **Stay Present and Focused**:
   - Avoid bringing up past issues during conversations, as this can complicate matters and detract from the current discussion.

3. **Engage Fully in Listening**:
   - Give your undivided attention to the speaker, refraining from formulating your response while they are speaking. This ensures you understand their perspective fully.

4. **Avoid Interruptions and Defensiveness**:
   - Refrain from interrupting the speaker, and resist the urge to become defensive if you disagree with their viewpoint. Allow them to express themselves fully before responding.

5. **Seek Solutions, Not Victories**:
   - Focus on finding mutually agreeable solutions rather than winning arguments. Collaborative problem-solving fosters effective communication and prevents conflict escalation.

6. **Take Breaks When Needed**:
   - If communication becomes tense or unproductive, take a break to relax and gather your thoughts before resuming the conversation.

7. **Consider Different Perspectives**:
   - Make an effort to understand the other person's viewpoint and be open to considering alternative solutions. Avoid dismissing ideas too quickly without fully understanding them.

8. **Respect Differing Opinions**:
   - Even if you disagree, show respect for the other person's perspective and listen attentively. Respectful communication builds trust and fosters constructive dialogue.

9. **Avoid Exaggeration and Blame**:
   - Refrain from exaggerating or blaming others during conversations. Instead, focus on expressing yourself truthfully and constructively to avoid escalating negativity.

10. **Take Responsibility and Analyze Objectively**:
   - Avoid placing blame solely on others and instead analyze conflicts objectively to find solutions. Taking responsibility fosters accountability and promotes effective communication.

36

10 Tips for Interview Success:

1. **Research the Company**:
   - Take time to research the company beforehand to understand their values, culture, and expectations. This knowledge can greatly enhance your interview performance and demonstrate your genuine interest.

2. **Present Yourself Professionally**:
   - Prepare for the interview by grooming yourself appropriately and selecting attire that aligns with the company culture and position you're applying for.

3. **Arrive Early**:
   - Aim to arrive at the interview location at least 10 minutes before the scheduled time to avoid feeling rushed and to demonstrate punctuality.

4. **Prepare Questions**:
   - Develop thoughtful questions to ask the interviewer, show-

casing your interest in the role and company. This demonstrates initiative and engagement.

5. **Make a Positive First Impression**:
   - Approach the interview with confidence, a friendly demeanor, and a firm handshake. First impressions are crucial, so exude professionalism from the moment you walk in.

6. **Show Genuine Interest**:
   - Express interest in the interviewer and inquire about their role within the company. Engaging in conversation shows your enthusiasm for the opportunity.

7. **Mind Your Body Language**:
   - Display confident body language throughout the interview, maintaining good posture and making eye contact. Positive body language reinforces your credibility and professionalism.

8. **Seek Clarification if Needed**:
   - Don't hesitate to ask for clarification if you're unsure about a question. It's better to seek clarity than to provide an inaccurate or incomplete response.

9. **Inquire About Follow-Up**:
   - Demonstrate your eagerness for the position by asking about the next steps in the hiring process and how and when you can expect to hear back.

10. **Express Interest in the Role**:

Conclude the interview by reiterating your enthusiasm for the position and highlighting your qualifications and what you can contribute to the company. Communicate your desire to join the team.

37

Chapter 6

Full Speed Ahead

38

Real-Life Applications of NLP (Neuro-Linguistic Programming.)

As the tale goes, Buddha was on his rounds seeking alms when someone verbally abused him. Buddha, being enlightened as he was, simply smiled and moved on. When a disciple asked how he could keep himself from retaliating against the extreme abuse, the Buddha observed that the evil words did not touch him or his philosophy of life. They only exposed the ignorance of the person saying it.

Of course, although the Buddha did not have the benefit of NLP in those days, he demonstrated how, due to his mental perception of the offensive as inoffensive, he remained unaffected by the abuse. However ancient the story, this is a prime example of how NLP can be applied to real-life situations. We rely on our sense perceptions to understand, interpret and interact with our environment.

NLP assigns a lot of importance to eye movements, observing and reading others' body language, and controlling our body language or gestures to communicate with others. Therefore, synchronizing your body language or non-verbal means of communication with verbal means enhances the effectiveness of your communication. Your choice of words and sentence structures delivered using the right tone can go a long way in casting a spell on the audience, convincing them, and bringing about desired outcomes through them. Your language, if used appropriately, can appeal to the subconscious mind of a hostile audience to obtain conscious compliance from them.

Influencing others' minds through a captivating speech to completely change moods and attitudes to achieve your desired result is not new. Still, NLP puts considerable emphasis on the techniques involved in the process. These techniques involve using your head position, eye movements, gestures, breathing rhythms, language, and visual and auditory senses.

Modeling Excellence

One of the applications of NLP is to do what is called "modeling excellence." When you recognize a genius or an exceptional person who can accomplish certain things or is excellent in a particular field, you may wish to use this person as a model. Through imitation, you can apply these same factors or qualities you admire in the person and apply them to yourself. NLP techniques aim to discover the most important elements that contribute to the person's excellence and transfer them to you so that you can replicate that excellence.

Therapeutic NLP

There are some therapeutic applications of NLP, which are mainly borrowed from the practice of hypnosis. These applications rely considerably on the terminology employed by an American psychiatrist, Milton H. Erickson, like hypnotic phenomena, therapeutic metaphor, story, rapport, age regression, conscious and unconscious communications, etc. Advocates of NLP believe that its techniques, especially those dealing with communication, can very well be applied in business for its promotion. One has first to master the NLP techniques and then skillfully use them to see the results for themselves.

39

Why You Need a Life Coach

If you want to achieve more or enhance your life, you should consider getting advice from a life coach. A life coach can be many things, including your consultant, someone who listens, or your manager. They can help set you in the right direction in life, help you to get the most out of life, determine your goals, and help you reach them.

Benefits of Having a Life Coach:

1. **Gain Control Over Your Life**:
   - A life coach can assist you in taking charge of your life and making decisions that align with your goals and values.

2. **Time Management Strategies**:
   - Develop effective time management techniques to prioritize tasks and achieve your objectives efficiently.

3. **Stress Reduction and Increased Productivity**:
   - Simplify your life and reduce stress by implementing

strategies recommended by your life coach, leading to enhanced productivity.

4. **Realize and Maximize Potential**:
   - Work with a life coach to identify your strengths, weaknesses, and areas for growth, allowing you to reach your full potential.

5. **Improved Relationships**:
   - Enhance your interpersonal skills and improve your relationships with others through guidance and support from a life coach.

6. **Task Prioritization and Deadline Management**:
   - Learn effective methods for prioritizing tasks and meeting deadlines, leading to increased efficiency and success.

7. **Support with Decision-Making**:
   - Receive assistance and guidance from your life coach when faced with important decisions in both your personal and professional life.

8. **Stress Management Techniques**:
   - Learn coping mechanisms and stress management techniques to navigate challenging situations with resilience and composure.

9. **Work-Life Balance**:
   - Achieve a healthy balance between your work and social life with the help of your life coach, ensuring overall well-being and fulfillment.

10. **Development of Action Plans and Life Goals**:
   - Collaborate with your life coach to establish clear action plans and set achievable life goals that align with your aspirations.

A life coach can provide valuable support and guidance in various aspects of your life, whether professional or personal, empowering you to achieve greater success and satisfaction. Through personalized strategies and a commitment to your growth, a life coach can help you unlock your full potential and improve your overall quality of life.

Do I Need a Life Coach?

To determine if you benefit from having a life coach, the first question you should ask yourself is, "What do I wish to accomplish with a life coach?" if you can answer this question, then a life coach would be able to work successfully alongside you to help you develop a strategy to obtain your goals. Life coaching is all about developing a partnership between the two of you, and you must be open to advice and constructive criticism; if you are not, then a life coach may not be the best option for you. Below are some questions that could help you determine if you could benefit from a life coach. If you can answer yes to any of them, you could benefit from having a life coach.

If you find yourself resonating with any of the following statements, it may be beneficial to seek support:

1. **Lack of Support**:
   - Do you feel there is a lack of support in your life, leaving you feeling isolated or unsupported?

2. **Low Self-Esteem Issues**:
   - Do you struggle with low self-esteem, impacting your confidence and self-worth?

3. **Lack of Clarity in Goals**:
   - Do you feel uncertain about your life's direction or lack clarity in setting goals for yourself?

4. **Need for Assistance**:
   - Are you going through a tough time and feel like you could benefit from a helping hand?

5. **Overwhelmed with Deadlines**:
   - Are you feeling overwhelmed with deadlines and unsure of how to manage your tasks effectively?

6. **Feeling Overwhelmed by Daily Tasks**:
   - Do the demands of daily tasks leave you feeling overwhelmed and unable to cope?

7. **Perception of External Pressure**:
   - Do you feel as though the world is against you, experiencing pressure from external sources?

8. **Perception of Missing Out on Success**:
   - Do you believe that everyone around you knows the secret to success, leaving you feeling left behind or inadequate?

9. **Desire for Self-Improvement**:
   - Do you feel that there is room for improvement in your life and a desire to better yourself or achieve more?

If any of these resonate with you, reaching out for support from friends, family, or a professional counselor or coach can be a valuable step toward addressing these challenges and finding greater fulfillment in your life. Remember, seeking help is a sign of strength, not weakness.

40

14 Indicators of Progress Towards Your Goals

Indicators of Progress Towards Your Goals:

1. **Deep Contentment and Happiness**:
   - Waking up each morning with a sense of excitement and anticipation for the day ahead signifies progress towards your desired state of contentment and happiness.

2. **Minor Signs of Progress**:
   - Recognizing smaller signs of progress can help reinforce your commitment to change, such as increased choices in clothing or a shift in mindset.

3. **Self-Improvement Goals**:
   - Whether you're aiming to lose weight, overcome addiction, boost self-esteem, or enhance communication skills, progress is evident in your efforts to better yourself.

4. **Patience and Persistence**:

- Acknowledge that changes take time and require patience. Progress may not be immediate, but consistent effort will yield results over weeks or months.

5. **Positive Self-Reflection**:
   - Noticing positive changes in yourself, such as smiling more in the mirror or feeling proud of your accomplishments, reflects progress towards self-acceptance and personal growth.

6. **Shift in Perspective**:
   - Embracing a mindset shift involves taking responsibility for your actions, letting go of blame, and prioritizing your own desires over others' expectations.

7. **External Validation**:
   - Feedback from others, such as compliments or observations about your transformation, reinforces your progress and motivates continued effort.

8. **Empowerment and Assertiveness**:
   - Progress is evident when you confidently assert your boundaries, say "no" when necessary, and prioritize your own needs and desires.

9. **Fearlessness and Confidence**:
   - Overcoming fears, making new friends, and feeling proud of your accomplishments signify increased confidence and fearlessness in pursuing your goals.

10. **Resilience and Adaptability**:
   - Learning from mistakes, laughing at setbacks, and bouncing

back more easily demonstrate resilience and adaptability in the face of challenges.

11. **Ease in Achieving Goals**:
   - Progress is evident when you find it easier to reach the goals you set for yourself and approach tasks with enthusiasm rather than procrastination.

12. **Natural Integration of Changes**:
   - Making positive changes to your life becomes second nature, indicating internalization and integration of new habits and behaviors.

13. **Consistent Positive Outlook**:
   - Feeling consistently optimistic and heading in the right direction signifies progress toward your desired state of well-being and fulfillment.

14. **Increased Sense of Purpose**:
   - Experiencing a heightened sense of purpose and direction in life is a clear indication of progress towards your goals, as it signifies alignment with your values and aspirations.

41

Moving on with Life

Sometimes, life has the habit of kicking us in the teeth, perhaps through no fault of our own. Things get tough, and we have periods of sorrow and hurt. This could be the death of a loved one, a breakup of a relationship, or sickness. We have two options to deal with what life throws at us: give up and go into depression or accept whatever happens and then move on with our lives. If we make the right choice, we grieve, pick ourselves up, and move on with our lives.

Bereavement

Bereavement comes to us all eventually in life. Sometimes it comes cruelly and strikes the young, while others are taken when they have lived out their years. However, whenever bereavement chooses to strike, it is just as heartbreaking for those left behind. Grieving will vary from person to person, and there isn't any hard limit on how much time we should or shouldn't suffer. There are also many stages to grieving, starting with shock, numbness, fear, and unsettlement, just a few of the many feelings that can flow through a person during this time.

Grieving, however, is a regular occurrence and significant occurrence if we are to get over this time and eventually move on with our lives. It is human nature's way of letting go, and you shouldn't try to hide any feelings or thoughts during this time. Having someone you can turn to, such as a family member or friend, can help significantly during your greatest time of need, and if you are lucky enough to have someone like this, you must take them up on their offer of being there for you.

Illness

Coping with a severe or life-threatening illness can be devastating; it can bring a range of emotional problems and physical disabilities. Finding that we or someone we love very much has a life-threatening or severe, catastrophic illness that brings fear, uncertainty, and even denial before true acceptance.

Denial to a degree is not necessarily a bad thing. If denial is used positively, it can help overcome problems to some degree and enable you to get back to living your life. However, total denial and not accepting at all is something entirely different. If this is the case, then you might need to seek help.

Break up of Relationships

The break up of any relationship can be traumatic, mainly if you have been together for many years or children are involved. Again, fear plays a big part; fear of what the future will bring, how you will cope, and feelings of betrayal and desertion all play an essential role. Time usually plays a crucial part in healing after a breakup. Grieving, to an extent, over what is essentially a loss helps to get your thoughts and feelings out. It enables you to move on with your life and take the next step forward into a new chapter.

42

Reflection

Throughout this book, we have explored various techniques, strategies, and insights aimed at empowering you to embark on a transformative journey within yourself. As you reflect on the concepts and exercises presented, remember that transformation is not an overnight process but rather a continuous journey of learning, growth, and evolution. It requires patience, persistence, and a willingness to embrace change.

By delving into your inner world, you have taken the first step towards unlocking your true potential, overcoming obstacles, and creating a life filled with purpose, meaning, and fulfillment. Whether you are seeking to improve your relationships, cultivate inner peace, or pursue your passions, the power to transform lies within you.

As you move forward on your journey, may you continue to nurture and cultivate your inner world with love, compassion, and mindfulness. Remember that each moment presents an opportunity for growth and that you have the ability to shape your reality according to your deepest desires.

Thank you for accompanying me on this transformative exploration. May your inner world continue to blossom and flourish, illuminating the path to a life of abundance, joy, and authenticity.